Ideas for
Coaching Your
Daughter's
4th-8th Grade
Basketball
Team

Never Forget They're Kids

MICHAEL O'HALLORAN

Book design by Johnson Design

Manufactured in the United States of America

Published by Brilliant & Bright, Inc.

Brilliant & Bright, Inc.
4146 Barrow
St. Paul, MN 55123

Library of Congress Cataloging-in-Publication Data

O'Halloran, Michael.

Never Forget They're Kids: Ideas for Coaching Your Daughter's
4th – 8th Grade Basketball Team / Michael O'Halloran.

ISBN 978-0-6151-5155-7

Also by Michael O'Halloran

Smart Attack® Baseball Trivia (audio CD)

Smart Attack® Basketball Trivia (audio CD)

Smart Attack® Football Trivia (audio CD)

Smart Attack® Sports Trivia (audio CD)

Designed for playing in the car or at home, these hands-free games can be played by one or many. Smart Attack Trivia Games challenge players to answer sports questions quickly. Along the way contestants learn about the game, teams, rules, terms, history, players and more. A brief musical interlude — about 5 seconds — plays after each question is read and before the answer is revealed.

The line is carried by ITunes and the Sports Trivia title won an "Editor's Pick" award from Audible.com.

http://smartattack.wordpress.com

For information, contact: mikeoh@comcast.net

Introduction

Coaching my fifth grade daughter's first game some years ago was my introduction to coaching traveling basketball. We played a tall and skilled team that had been playing together for some time. Having had no practices, our players barely knew everyone's names and were still coming to grips with the rule changes allowing double-teaming and pressure after defensive rebounds. The other team opened in a full-court zone press, and we were down 20 points in no time. Things didn't improve much after that.

As a coach, I wasn't quite prepared for that type of "total immersion" schooling. I vowed I'd be better prepared for future games.

I've put together this book to share with new coaches some of my ideas in hopes that you won't be caught as unprepared as I was for your first season. Perhaps veteran coaches may find something of interest in here as well. It's a grab bag of planning suggestions, quotes, practice ideas and my opinions on coaching kids.

I should note that as the father of four daughters, most of my coaching experience has been with girls. Some of the ideas that follow may apply to boys' teams; and some may not. I hope you find this to be a useful tool.

One of the most useful pieces of advice I received on coaching basketball came from an old coach who had just finished a practice while I was about to start my first with a team of 5th graders. When I asked if he had any words of wisdom, he told me I'd do just fine if I remembered this thought, "Never Forget They're Kids."

Coaching kids' teams can be a very rewarding experience. Have fun!

– Michael O'Halloran

P.S. Please send me your comments about this book to mikeoh@comcast.net

Contents

ONE Planning the Season

Spend a good chunk of timing thinking through how you'd like to see the season go. Some things to consider:

The Importance of Recruiting Assistant Coaches

The most important piece of advice I can give new coaches is to recruit great assistant coaches. It can be a long season. Assistants can fill in when you're gone and help you when you're there. Having two assistants for a team gets the player/instructor ratio down to about 3-1 for most teams. This allows for more personalized instruction that can yield great results. If you can recruit at least 2 assistants, you're in good shape. Coaching is very similar to the real world — if you have the right people in place; it makes all the difference.

Recruit, cajole and beg to get the right people in place. It matters.

Meet with your assistants and share your coaching approach. Discuss your expectations for them and your plan for the season.

"There are really only two plays: Romeo and Juliet, and put the darn ball in the basket."
—Abe Lemons

Do Some Research

There are lots of good resources to turn to learn more about coaching basketball.

Books

If you're only going to read one book, the one to read is: <u>Wooden: A Lifetime of Observations and Reflections On and Off the Court</u>. John Wooden won 10 national championships in 12 years at UCLA, and is the coach most people recognize as the best who ever lived. After reading this book, you'll quickly realize the championships didn't happen by accident. The book is a quick read, full of short tenets and teachings that he

"It's what you learn after you know it all that counts."
—John Wooden

compiled over the years. You'll likely see many applications not only for your basketball coaching, but also for life.

There are a lot of good books out there on coaching basketball. (See Attachment A for a list of book, web site and videos on basketball coaching)

> *"It's not what you tell your players that counts. It's what they hear."*
> **—Red Auerbach**

Web Sites

Basketball web sites can provide a wealth of information for coaches. If your team needs a new inbounds play, go to www.degerstrom.com. Having a hard time understanding the flex offense go to www.members.tripod.com/~coacheshome/play.html to see an animated diagram. These sites and others can help you throughout the season.

Other Coaches

Talk to other basketball coaches. Make a point to ask them about their experiences. What's worked and what hasn't? Ask them how they run their practices. What drills work? What type of offense do they run? Which defenses have worked best?

Observe other coaches and teams in practices and games and see what works. Go to a coaching clinic if you can. All of my favorite practice drills and game plays, I've learned from somewhere else: a book, a web site, another coach, watching another team practice, etc. The sport of basketball has been around long enough that there just isn't that much that's new anymore.

Think Through Team Goals and Plan Your Approach:

Spend some time now to plan your interactions with your team. Even if you coached many years before, I think it's a valuable exercise.

By way of example, here are the goals I set one year.

> **What do I hope each player walks away with after playing this season?**
>
> - Increased confidence in their basketball skills: both team and individual.
>
> - A positive experience and some friendships.
>
> - A knowledge of some of the life lessons that the sport can teach:
>
>   – Hard work and purpose lead to success.
>
>   – A willingness to take chances because that's how we grow and get better.
>
>   – Winning and losing with grace.
>
>   – The power and magic of teamwork – everyone can make a difference.

Basketball Focus

- Focus on skills that are important to the game that players will be able to utilize with future teams in the coming years. For example, understanding: a team defense approach, how to box out, pick-and-rolls, give-and-gos, backdoor cuts to the basket, correct shooting form, dribbling with both hands, etc.

"What does this program/team need this week?"

–Dick Bennett

- Balance the importance of repetition to learn skills with keeping it fresh.

- Create multi-dimensional players: centers will know how to dribble and guards will know how to rebound.

- Defense creates offense.

- Our team will have few plays, but lots of know-how.

- Place an emphasis on quality practices. Most other teams will practice the same types of things that we practice. But, our knowledge of the details and level of execution will set us apart.
- Focus on teaching players not correcting referees.

Keys to My Approach

- **Be positive.** Kids accomplish the most when they feel confident.
- **Breakdown complicated activities** into bite-size chunks.
- **Encourage a risk-taking environment.** The effort needs to be rewarded even with the result is lacking.
- **Empower players to think on their own.**
- **Never forget they're kids.**

"Players need to learn how to play without the ball and without the coach."

—Pete Carril

• *Basketball is not the only thing in kids' lives.*

Basketball can be a big commitment — two practices and two game days a week (and sometimes more). If a player misses a practice to go skiing, don't sweat it. If they'd prefer to go see the school play one night, good for them.

> *"What you are as a person is far more important than what you are as a basketball player."*
> —John Wooden

When I compare how many games my daughter plays in one season to how many I played as a grade-schooler, it's staggering. She probably played more games in one season than I did in three seasons. A few missed practices and games is probably a healthy thing for many players — especially those in multiple traveling sports.

Try to read the mood of your players at each practice. Based on their energy levels, time of day and other factors; some practices may lend themselves to teaching a complicated technique better than others. Relax and pull back when needed.

• *The way kids define success for their basketball experience may not involve looking at their team's won-loss record.*

In a pre-season survey of 5th grade girls, I asked the players what their goals were for the year. Nearly every player listed "having fun" or some variation and most indicated that they wanted to "get better' or some variation. Interestingly, no one listed "win five 1st place trophies" or some "win-loss record" or anything to do with wins.

When polled three-quarters of the way through the year on what they liked best about traveling basketball, most said "the games and the team get-togethers." Note, it wasn't "winning games" but just "the games." "Eating at restaurants" and "being able to play point guard" both had strong showings.

13

In both polls, the players seemed right on with their priorities—having fun and player development were priorities.

- *Plan events and mini-events to keep things fresh and to let kids be kids.*

As a coach, I was always amazed at how sometimes the simplest of events, e.g., "Sock Day" at practice (wear your wildest socks), were things that the players really looked forward to and talked about.

The next page lists some activities that our team or other teams have done to keep things interesting and fun. Use them on occasion or come up with some events of your own.

Some Ideas to Keep Kids Interested

1) **"Hoosiers" movie and pizza party at coach's house:** Kids are much more comfortable and feel better about things when they know everyone on the team.

   An informal setting allows players more time to talk and get to know each other. Watch *Hoosiers* or another movie to kick off the season.

2) **"It's a Game" practice:** Before the first game or scrimmage, schedule an inter-squad game. Have the players wear their uniforms to practice and walk through the entire practice as if it were a game — only stopping action to make teaching points. Assign a coach to each squad, run through pre-game warm-ups, play 4 quarters, etc. Lots of questions may come up, e.g. where do we stand for the jump ball? Players should feel more comfortable after this walk-through come time for the real game.

3) **Rock n' roll practice:** A boom box and some lively music can jazz up any boring practice. Little Bow Wow's *"Playing Basketball"* was a favorite with our team.

4) **Hat Day:** Wear your favorite hat to practice. Give out small prizes for the most creative, hat-you-couldn't-give-away, etc.

5) **Sock Day:** Perhaps the most looked-forward to event of the year for our fifth grade girls' team. Go figure.

6) **Parent/child game:** You'll discover quickly where the kids got their competitive genes. If a child's parent can't make it, have them invite an older friend or sibling.

7) **Shooting Contest day:** Players are challenged in a series of fun games: Around the World, free-throw contest, 3-point contest, etc.

8) **Slam Dunk Photo Session:** Borrowed from a scene in the movie "Hoop Dreams," have coaches stack wrestling mats or bring a table near a hoop lowered to 8 feet. Allow each player to pose doing their favorite slam-dunks — with ball above the rim — while a coach or a parent takes photos. A spotter may be needed to prevent falls. Show photos at the next practice.

Examples of a slam dunk photo session.

9) **Basketball quiz:** Pass out some info on the history of basketball, player info, rules, team plays, etc., at one practice. Have a short quiz with a prize for the top score at the next. I think nearly everyone on our team could tell you whom the first woman was to dunk in a professional basketball game. (Lisa Leslie)

10) **Holiday gift exchange:** Let the kids orchestrate.

THREE Meet the Parents

The old saying that "the best team to coach is the team from the orphanage" can sometimes have merit. But, it doesn't have to be the case. Here are some ways to get off on the right foot with parents:

1. Get folks talking right away. As with the kids, the sooner they become comfortable with each other, the sooner the shared good times. Plan an introduction exercise. For example, "We're going to go around the room and I'd like everyone to make a short introduction: name, daughter's name, other siblings, etc. Also, please share with us a memorable sports moment from your childhood." As the coach, you begin.

2. Outline your expectations for parents. Here are a few things you might include:

   • When your daughter is going to miss a game or practice, ideally please have her let me know or you can let me know in person, by phone or e-mail.

   • If at any time during the season you have questions or concerns about how things are going, playing time, approach, etc.; please let me know.

   • Support and respect the officiating. Set a good example for the players.

   • Appreciate good effort (good hustle!) and achievement (great pass!); but please do not provide instruction from the sidelines (Shoot!).

> "I've come to the frightening conclusion that I am the decisive element in the classroom. It's my daily mood that makes the weather. As a teacher, I possess a tremendous power to make a child's life miserable or joyous. I can be a tool of torture or an instrument of inspiration. I can humiliate or humor, hurt or heal. In all situations, it is my response that decides whether a crisis will be escalated or de-escalated and a child humanized or de-humanized."
>
> —Dr. Haim Ginott

- Most kids want their parents at games, appreciative of good play from both teams, but otherwise fairly quiet.

3. Consider providing some suggestions for interacting with players after the game:

- If you miss your child's game, the first questions you ask are indications to the child as to what you consider to be the most important parts of the game. Perhaps "how many points did you score?" shouldn't always be the first question. Consider: "How did you play?" or "Did you have fun out there?" or "Did you make any good passes?" What you deem important, your child will.

- I don't know many people who like to be told everything they did wrong or could've done better immediately after playing a game. Pick and choose your times to make suggestions. Especially in the immediate post-game excitement, words of encouragement work best.

- Consider the sandwich compliment approach:
  Part 1: communicate a sincere compliment on something your child's done well ("You had some great rebounds!")
  Part 2: After the reaction, make a suggestion for a way to improve ("for next time, you may want to consider dribbling more with your left hand to avoid ending up in the right-hand corner")
  Part 3: Followed by another compliment ("You were creating a lot of trouble for the other team with your tough defense. Great Job!") By wrapping a suggestion between two compliments, you may find a more receptive audience.

FOUR Show Time: Your First Meeting With Players

For your first meeting with the players, here are some ideas:

- Players' interviews and introductions: Pair players off with someone they don't know. Both players are challenged to interview the other and introduce her at the next practice. Sample questions you might encourage players to ask include: What's your favorite subject at school? Tell me about your siblings and pet? What other sports and hobbies do you have?

- Recruit some older players tell about their experiences in travel ball: This can be particularly effective for first year travel players.

- 15 minutes before practice rule: During the first part of the season, there's a lot to cover to get players up to speed for the first games. For each practice, many coaches require players to come 10 - 15 minutes early. It's a great time to cover a wide spectrum of topics. It allows time for players to ask questions. As the season progresses, this time may be shortened.

- Poll your players: What are their expectations? Likes and dislikes? Why do they play? What would they like to improve on? What makes a good coach? What makes a player enjoyable to coach? Get a feel for what's going through players' minds at the start of the season.

Develop a Team Identity

Create a name for your team. Challenge your players to come up with a name.

Visit www. International basketball.com/teamnames.html for a list of basketball team nicknames.

Basket hounds and Shooting Stars were names that players came up with on their own.

18

- Outline your expectations for the players: Some coaches' expectations include: be on time for practices and games, try your hardest, and be a team player. These are all fair expectations.

  My expectations for players can be condensed to one word: respect. I expect players to show respect for:

  - Officials
  - Opponents
  - Coaches
  - Teammates
  - Their parents
  - And the game

The "respect" expectation is broad enough to cover a wide array of situations. If a player is constantly late to practices without letting the coach know, the player is not showing respect to the coaches or teammates. If players are not taking practice serious, they're not showing respect for the game.

FIVE Practice Plans

At the start of the season, there are many directions a coach can take a team in hopes of preparing players for the first games.

My approach is based on two premises:

- Defense and rebounding wins games, and
- Defense creates offense. Open looks for shots at the basket are critical. Defensive turnovers create open looks.

Because of this, my early practices focus on:

- Team defense
- Man-to-man defense &
- Rebounding

For my practices, I usually follow a "meat and potatoes" approach. For any given practice, I focus on two main subjects that are essential for player development.

For the "meat", or main course, I set aside 30 - 35 minutes, the longest segment of the practice. This segment is covered early in the practice while the kids are still fresh. In my first three practices of the year the meat topics were: team defense, man-to-man defense and rebounding.

"We are what we repeatedly do. Excellence then is not an act, but a habit."
—Aristotle

My Biggest Mistake
With my first team, the biggest mistake I made was trying to do too much too soon. Better to have a team learn a few of the really important fundamentals cold, than to expose them to a lot, and not allow enough time for the material to be learned.

"No rebounds - no rings."
—Pat Riley

For the "potatoes" portion of practice, I set aside about 15 - 20 minutes. Important topics like "how to set a screen" or "how to get open without the ball."

Before, between and after these two features, shorter drills and topics are covered.

Topics addressed in both the "meat" and "potatoes" sections are important enough that they need to be reinforced in subsequent practices and throughout the year. Repetition is critical for learning.

The pace of the practices is fairly quick. We move from one exercise to another to maximize our use of the gym time and keep interest levels high.

If you're practicing at a facility that has multiple hoops, put them to use. I always asked that every player bring their own ball to practice. Players could use the team balls when they forgot. But with each player having a ball to themselves, it was easy to do dribbling and shooting drills.

See Attachment B for a Sample Practice Plan.

More Stuff

- Don't spend too much time talking during practice. Kids want to play. Get the players running, dribbling and shooting early in the practice to burn off some excess energy before trying to spend any length of time trying to talk to the team on the court. Players tend to be less disruptive when they're catching their breath.

> **Post-it!**
> Post-it Notes make a great coaching aid. Use them to mark starting positions and other areas on the courts for drills, e.g. for a jump-stop lay-up you should be shooting here — right in front of this post-it note. Also, use them to jot down notes for next practices.

- Balance providing some consistency in practice with mixing it up to keep it fresh. For consistency, at nearly every practice our team executed two drills: jump stop lay-ups and dribble waves. Both drills taught skills important to the team's success. Also, by consistently running these same two drills, it was a great way to judge individual and team progress throughout the year.

> *"Shout praise and whisper criticism."*
> *–Don Meyer*

- Create some mini-competitions at practices. It's a great way of keeping everyone's interest during repetitive drills. Divide your team into two groups and challenge them to see which can make the most lay-ups in two minutes.

- It's a great practice to highlight kids who are doing a particular drill well and let them demonstrate it in front of the whole team. It can be a great boost to players' self-esteem. Try to make sure each kid gets a chance to do this before the end of the season.

- Whatever the age group, it never hurts to go over the fundamentals: dribbling, passing, shooting form, pivoting (seldom taught enough), rebounding, driving to the basket, cutting, defensive stance, defensive slide, hustling back on defense, denying the pass, ball-side defense, help-side defense, and communicating on defense.

- Learn from John Wooden who isn't a big fan of "Killers" or "30-second drills" unless the players are dribbling. Players can get a great workout through a series of other drills during practice.

- Another Wooden concept: try to end every practice on a high note. It might be a shooting contest or drill, but make it one that most players find fun.

"What do I do on offense when I don't have the ball?"

A first year player posed this question to me after her first shift in her first game. It's a great question because most of the time on offense — 80% of the time if possession time was equal — a player doesn't have the ball.

After muddling through the answer at the time, I now work through the "I'm a SPORT" mnemonic device with players at practices.

I'M A SPORT	
I = Eye	Keep your eye on the ball at all times.
M = Movement	You're nearly always moving on offense. It's not random movement, but movement with a purpose. Move decisively.
A = Alert	Be alert for opportunities.
S = Spacing	Keep your spacing, don't bunch up and make it easy for the defense. About 15 feet apart is a good distance. Just say "no" to the right-hand corner bunch-up.
P = Picks	Set picks to free the player with the ball, but also set picks to get people open. Remember that frequently it's the picker off a roll that is open for shots.
O = Open	Work to get open. Cut to the basket, cut across the paint, v-cut and look for passes. Timing is critical.
R = Rebound	Get yourself in a position to rebound a shot. Remember that most rebounds go to the opposite side of the rim from the shooter. Long shots create longer rebounds.
T = Trouble	Look to see if the ball handler has picked up the dribble. If the ball handler is in trouble, look to help.

SIX Defense

Three things you'll want your players to know

1. **Team defense:** Understand ball-side and weak-side defense. Understand the implications of the player she's covering having the ball, being a pass-away and being two passes-away as it relates to their positioning on the court. Good team defense minimizes open looks at the basket. A team that plays great team defense and can rebound will do well in most games.

> *"I hate it. It looks like a stickup at 7-Eleven. Five guys standing there with their hands in the air."*
> —Norm Sloan, on zone defense

2. **Man-to-man defense:** When playing in the summer or for fun during the season, the focus for most players is offense-minded. Encourage your players to be defense-minded. Being able to play good man-to-man defense is a skill that translates to every team your players will go on to. Teach it early and often.

3. **A pressing defense:** Being able to run an effective pressing defense, be it man-to-man or zone defense, is very important. A pressing defense creates turnovers that create open looks that create points. For fifth and sixth grade teams, the full-court pressure that a 1-2-1-1 zone press delivers can create havoc. Other pressing defenses can be equally effective. Since ball-handling skills are not advanced at these grade levels, creating pressure the entire length of the court creates many opportunities for the offensive team to turn the ball over. If the turnover happens early, your team doesn't have a great distance to go to get off a shot.

> *"False Hustle = cheap fouls, lunging, reaching, etc."*
> —Billy Donovan

By practicing your own zone press in practice, it prepares you offensively for teams that press you. To learn how to break the press on offense, you need to practice with a team that knows how to press. Who better than your own team? I also find a pressing defense to be great for conditioning. Kids get used to the level of energy and thinking needed to apply the pressure on defense and break the pressure on offense. While they may encounter different types of zone defense against different teams, by learning one zone defense, they can apply many of the concepts they've learned in order to break the press.

Some rebounding coaching points

• **Location:** Get to the right spot on the floor. Two-thirds of rebounds go to the opposite side of the rim of the shooter. Long shots create long rebounds.

• **Technique:** Stop, Drop & Hop. "Stop" the person your defending by boxing out, "Drop," get lower and ready to jump, and "Hop" to the ball by jumping or running to get there.

• **Desire:** Some of the best rebounders are not the tallest folks on the court. A lot of success in rebounding comes from wanting the ball.

SEVEN

Offense

Some considerations

- **Overall approach:** In most situations, encourage your players to shoot the ball the first time they have the ball in good shooting range and can get off the shot. This minimizes the opportunities for turnovers. Also, other players know that when a teammate has an open look in shooting range, to get in place for rebounds. "Good shooting range" will vary from player to player.

- **Teach a number system and establish a basic offensive set or two.** In our offense, #1 is the point guard, #2 is the shooting guard, #3 & #4 are forwards and #5 is the center. Establish some basic sets so players start off correctly and are properly spaced. For example, a 1-4 low set, places the point guard at the top of the key with the ball; 3 & 5 are on the left side and 2 & 4 are on the right side.

- **Focus on fundamentals:** the following three offensive skills are essential. We work on them in nearly all practices and use drills to reinforce them in warm-ups before games.

  1. Give-and-go

  2. Cut to the basket and cut to get open

  3. Pick-and-roll

It's important that players know these concepts inside and out. For example, to teach the pick-and-roll, go into great detail: how wide to set your feet, how much space between the defender to set it up, where to place your hands, what angle to set the pick, picking for players without the ball, executing the roll footwork from both sides, which way to roll, how the ball handler sets up the pick, how to run the defender into the pick, how close to run off the pick, etc.

- Running the offense and set plays: At the fifth grade level, it makes sense to have a few set plays to use. It exposes players to the discipline of running a play properly and if the plays work, it creates great scoring opportunities. Try executing the plays in games when you can. Some defenses are easier to run plays against than others. It's important that kids know how to freelance when no play is called. Some suggestions on running set plays:

1. Give definitive directions as to exactly where you want players to begin and move to during the play. Even if the player isn't intended to touch the ball in the designated play, give them a route to take to get the rebound.

2. The timing of when players move is also critical. If a player breaks to soon, by the time the ball handler wants to make the pass, the player is covered. Use "when the dribbler picks up the dribble" as a signal for when the first pass receiver makes the break to get open.

3. Have a back-up plan. If the play is foiled, what should the person with the ball do?

4. Consistent practice of plays is needed. Practice some of the plays in warm-ups right before the game to make sure the players remember what to do.

5. Good teams quickly figure out "clear outs" and plays that focus on only one player touching the ball. But, if there's too many passes to get the play off the ground, there's a lot of opportunities for turnovers. Keep passes to a minimum to optimize your chances for success.

6. The most successful play we ran — The Special — usually entailed only two passes. The play is essentially a give-and-go. It was simple and every player knew exactly her role. In more than one game, this one play accounted for about 1/3 of our entire point total. See Attachment C for a diagram of the play.

- **Teaching shooting form:** Until players gain a certain level of strength, it's difficult for them to consistently shoot with the correct form. But, the earlier you can expose them to the right form, the better. See Attachment D for some more tips on shooting form.

I think the two biggest shooting errors for 4th – 8th graders are:

Incorrect form —Note how elbow bends out when ball is centered on body.

1. **The Flying Elbow** The flying elbow is the name given to shooting when the elbow of the shooting arm is outside of the ball instead of underneath it. An incorrect starting position with the ball is often the root cause. Shooters will incorrectly center the ball with their body, which forces the elbow out when shooting. This is especially true with younger players who need the power of both arms just to reach the basket.

Correct form—Note how elbow is under the ball.

To correct this, the starting position of the ball, the pocket, should be to the right of the temple or slightly lower for an 8th grade right-handed shooter. A fifth grader's shooting pocket might be waist level or slightly lower. By having the ball in the correct starting position, the player will have a better opportunity to keep the elbow in line. Make frequent use of the "Look Ma, One Hand" shooting drill described in the "Driveway Work Out" (see Attachment E). This drill makes it very difficult for a shooter to center the ball on the body when beginning to shoot.

"We have a great bunch of outside shooters. Unfortunately, all our games are played indoors.

–Weldon Drew

28

2. Shooting with too low of an arc —
The optimal arc for the flight of a
basketball — 42 to 48 degrees — is
higher than at what most players
shoot. By increasing the arc, players
increase their chances of making
baskets.

The elbow of the shooting
arm (right elbow if you're
right-handed) should
finish above eye-level.

• **Zone offense:** When you encounter half-
court zone defenses like a 2-3 or
a 1-3-1, you'll want your players to:

1. Have an awareness that the other
team is playing zone defense and
that some of their offensive
playmaking that's effective when
going against a man-to-man defense
may not be going against a zone.

2. Understand the importance of the
offensive set. Take advantage of the
weaknesses of the zone defense
being played against you. If they
have two players out top on defense,
you'll likely start with 3 on offense
— a point and two wings. You may
want to overload one side against a
2-3. If they're in a 1-3-1 and have
one person out on top, you'll have
two on top.

If the elbow finishes below
eye-level, the shot has too
low of an arc.

3. Against a zone, teach your players to: know the value of quick
passing over dribbling to attack a zone, draw two defenders to
the ball handler and then find an open teammate, find holes in
the defense, understand that strong offensive rebounding can
cripple the zone, skip pass for open shots, etc.

- **Importance of in-bound plays:** When your team has the ball under your basket for a in-bound throw-in, it's a great opportunity to get a player an open look for a shot. Since many games at young ages end with low scores (14 –12) one or two made shots from in-bound plays can be critical. Don't hesitate to use a time-out before the in-bound plays to remind everyone of assignments and how the play works. These situations might sometimes be your best scoring opportunities in games or come at very critical times in the game when you really need a basket.

Consider having at least 3-4 inbound plays to take advantage of these opportunities. At least one play should be a viable option for when a team plays a 2-3 defense against you. See Attachment F or a diagram of inbounds play "23" to be used against a zone defense. See Attachment G for a diagram of inbounds play "Pizza" to be used against a man-to-man defense.

EIGHT Game Time

- John Wooden's philosophy about coaching from the bench during the game: "You teach during practice and games are a measure of how far you've taught your students. " It's difficult to win or lose games from the bench during games. If a team is underperforming during a game, it's more likely than not that they haven't been prepared properly.

Want to make life difficult for an opposing coach and team? Switch your defenses during stops in play or with made baskets. Going from a zone full-court defense to a half-court press and back again will challenge many offensive teams.

- Pre-game talks. Because kids are naturally excited for games, coaches generally don't need to say much to get them up for games. I think it's a good idea to try to keep kids calm and focused. Consider reminding them of how hard they've worked and perhaps say something to instill confidence before the game. People perform better when they're confident of their abilities.

- Let the players be the stars. If you're standing up more than 5 minutes during the game, you're probably standing up too much. Sit down. Parents and fans come to watch the players, not the coach.

- Use of time outs. In addition to try to slowing down runs by the other team and pointing out teaching opportunities, you'll want to consider using your time-outs for when your players are in trouble with the ball. I called timeouts on occasion to try to avoid 10-second calls, when our player was double-teamed in a corner, etc. When one or two baskets so often decide games, one turnover avoided can be big.

- Don't take a player out of the game because of a mistake. I've talked to some coaches who think it's a wise practice to pull a kid out of a game after a turnover or mistake she's made, just for a minute or until the next time out, to give some words of advice in hopes of preventing a future, similar error. I think it's a bad idea. Despite good intentions, the coach is isolating the player by substituting only for her and I don't know of any kids who like that. If it's some game saving advice you need to deliver, and it can't wait until the standard substitution time — remember many kids are playing only 3 1/2 minutes shifts — call a time out, or substitute in bigger numbers. Even if kids say it doesn't bother them, it does. Let them play through their mistakes.

- Dealing with bad officiating. I find it helps to go in with very low expectations. If the refs are good, you'll be pleasantly surprised. If not, well, you got what you expected.

  Engaging in an on-going negative commentary with the referees is a bad path to take for these reasons:

  - It seldom helps and frequently hurts your team.
  - It sets a poor example for the players.
  - You become a poor representative for your community.
  - It distracts you from your primary purpose of helping develop your players' basketball skills.

"The rule was "No autopsy, no foul."

—Stewart Granger, on the pickup games of his childhood

When players point out referees' mistakes, e.g. "I was fouled and the ref didn't call it", try pointing out that no one is perfect. "We've missed some shots, we've made some bad passes, we've made some coaching errors — in the same way, referees can't be expected to be right all the time."

If you feel compelled to talk to the referees during the game, talk to them in a way you'd like to be talked to. Wait for a break in the action, do it quietly and take the emotion out of it.

Unprofessional behavior by the referees should be reported to the tournament officials. A pattern of poor officiating in a game can also be reported to tournament officials. Usually the best you can hope for is that you don't run into the same bad officials again.

- Post-game congratulations. In the "winning and losing with grace" category, teach your players the three components that make up a good post-game congratulation.

The three parts are:

1. Look the other player in the eye.

2. Shake hands, high-five, go knuckle-to-knuckle or some variation.

3. Offer a sincere compliment to at least one player, maybe the one you were guarding.

Players should be taught the sign of a true champion is handling winning and losing with equal grace. Acting like your dog died after a team loss is not the best demonstration of good sportsmanship.

- Post-game talks. When in doubt, ask your audience for input. Ask your players what they think they did well and what they think they need to work on. Try the compliment sandwich approach with your team: something good, something they need to work on and then something good again. For the "something they need to work" part, don't dwell on it too long right after the game. Save it for the next practice. For fun, have players submit their votes for the play-of-the-game.

  "Don't coach mad."
  —Rick Pitino

- On keeping individual stats. While tracking statistics like steals, rebounds, assists, etc., can be a valuable coaching aid, I'm not a big fan of broadcasting them to players on a regular basis. The negatives I've seen from this practice greatly outweigh any potential benefits. The focus should be on team achievements, not individual achievements. Try highlighting one or two individual achievements of players, sometimes using stats, at the season-ending party. Even then, try to avoid apples-to-apples comparisons so that the players with the lowest point or rebound totals don't feel bad.

NINE

Some Other Things to Consider

- **Notifying players of their team selection.** In addition to talking to the parents to give them the agenda and other information, make a point to talk to the player directly. Think of any good things they did in try-outs and tell them when you get them on the line.

> *"Hearing improves with PRAISE!"*
> –Mark Gottfried

- **Stay in touch with players' parents.** E-mail is a great tool for keeping team parents in the loop. Set up the group mailing list early and communicate often.

I believe that early in the season, kids are kind of wondering how they're doing. Think of yourself on a first job. There's a natural curiosity to know if others think you're doing a good job. Let them know. In addition to letting players know their doing a great job at practices, I've found it valuable to send a short note to the parents highlighting a couple of the reasons their daughter has been valuable to the team, and I ask them to share this with their daughters. My sense is that there's more power to the compliments when it's coming from both parents and the coach.

- **Coaching your own kid.** Coaching your own child can be a very rewarding experience but is not without some challenges. Try to avoid the two most common errors.

The first is being too rough on your kid because she's your kid and you think she can handle it. Sometimes the thought process is that by being hard on your own daughter, you're setting an example for the whole team. Any accusations of favoritism can be avoided. But, it's not fair to your own kid.

A second common error is when coaches give their own kid preferential treatment. Maybe they believe there should be some reward for all of the time they put into coaching. Or, they believe their child is more talented than others, when actual play might indicate otherwise. This approach is not fair to the other players.

Your challenge is to try to coach your own daughter like you coach the other players on your team. Try to spend the same amount of one-on-one time in practice with her as you do with the other players. Not less, not more. Treat her the same as other players.

Know when to wear your parent hat and when to wear your coach's hat. If your child is hurt bad on the court — wear your parent hat. If your child wants to create the starting line-ups — wear your coach's hat. Car rides home from games are good times to wear the parent hat.

In the long run, your child will appreciate being treated equally as a part of the team.

- **Recognize your players individually at the season-ending party.** As the years go by, the trophies may be sitting in some box in the garage or even given away to make room, but kids will still remember the kind words a coach used to recognize them in front of their peers and parents.

Create your own team awards for the season ending party.

- **Thank your support team** — For most teams, a lot of people end up contributing to the effort. Perhaps you'll have scorekeepers, a team parent, assistants for scheduling practices and tournaments, and more Recognize their efforts. Thank them for their contributions.

Attachment A

Recommended Reading, Viewing and Gear

Books

Any book by John Wooden

The Baffled Parent's Guide to Coaching Youth Basketball, David G. Faucher

Five-Star Basketball Coaches' Playbook, Leigh Klein

Blackboard Strategies: Over 200 Favorite Plays From Successful Coaches For Nearly Every Possible Situation, Eric Sacharski

Coaching Girls' Basketball: From the How-To's of the Game to Practical Real-World Advice--Your Definitive Guide to Successfully Coaching Girls, Sandy Simpson

Coaching Youth Basketball: The Guide for Coaches & Parents (Betterway Coaching Kids Series), John P. McCarthy Jr.

Web sites

Basketball Highway — Check out the "ask the coach" and "ask the shooting pro" sections @ www.bbhighway.com

The Coach's Clipboard — Offensive and defensive strategies and more @ www.coachesclipboard.net/index.shtml

Coach's Notebook — A wide variety of topics covered from managing blowouts to managing superstars @ www.akcoach.com/

Coach your kids — Learn the principles of the Triangle offense for kids and more @ www.coachyourkids.com

Degerstrom — Over 800 free drills broken down by category @ www.degerstrom.com/basketball/

Tripod — See Shock Wave animation of the Kentucky offense, the Duke defense and the Flex offense @ www.members.tripod.com/~coacheshome/play.html

Attachment A, continued

Video

Steve Alford on Shooting

Forrest Larson's "Take it to the Rim" series

Gear

- Dribbling glasses — One-size fits all glasses that don't allow the ball handler to look down at the ball. Dribblers learn to control ball by touch and feel. Especially effective for 4th and 5th graders.

- Jay Wolf's Basketball Shooting Strap — Designed by physical education teacher and professional shooting coach Jay Wolf to eliminate the reason many players shoot poorly — using two hands to push the ball. The shooting strap requires that players develop a one-hand release, which is a key to developing a reliable shot. Jay's shooting strap, worn on the non-shooting hand, restricts movement of that arm forcing players to use the proper one-hand release. Jay Wolf's Basketball Shooting Strap can be found at many basketball merchandise web sites.

- Medicine kit — Plan on including items like ice packs, band-aids, tape (for jammed fingers) and other medical care items.

- Miscellaneous items — You'll also want to store the following items either in the kit or in your ball bag: pencils, post-it notes, whistle, dry-erase board and marker for playmaking from the bench, and a hand pump with needles.

- Copies of your team roster — Include the jersey numbers and list in ascending order. These can be quickly handed to the official scorekeeper and the opposing team's scorekeeper at the start of the game so that you or an assistant don't have to take the time to fill in the same info each time.

Attachment B

Sample Practice Plan

MINUTES	ACTIVITY
0 – 5	*Warm up* by dribbling up and down the court at a comfortable pace, first right-handed, then left-handed.
5 – 15	*Dribbling wave drills.* Starting in the corner of one baseline, player dribbles left-handed to middle of free-throw, does a cross-over dribble and dribbles right-handed to the intersection of half-court and the out-of-bound line. Dribbler proceeds zig-zagging down the court to the next free throw line, and then on to the intersection of the baseline and out-of-bounds line, and then dribbles all the way back around the outside of the court. The first time or two, the cross-over dribble is used as the transition. The next time, the transition dribble is a reverse dribble (some folks call it a spin dribble). Next, the transition is one-step-back, then cross-over (sometimes called the Butch Lee, a player who was very adept at this maneuver) Then, the transition is between-the-legs. Then, behind-the-back. We didn't always use the latter two, but it's a good stretch goal for some teams.

Water Break

15 – 45	**THE MEAT: THE PRIMARY FOCUS OF THE PRACTICE** *Team Defense:* Demonstrate with coaches and player volunteers, Divide into two teams and practice. Stop play after passes to see if players are learning the concept. Drill on calling out picks and playing defense against them.
45 – 55	*5 person weave* — on the way back, shooter and passer are on defense in a 3-on-2 drill.

Attachment B, continued

Water Break

55 – 65   ***Jump-stop lay-ups competition***

65 – 80   **THE POTATOES: THE SECONDARY FOCUS OF THE
PRACTICE**
"No Dribble" Scrimmage. Focus for offense is getting
open with v-cuts and picks, squaring up, and making
good passes. Focus for the defense is working through
picks, communicating and looking to create turnovers.

80 – 85   ***Mikan Drill.*** How many shots can players make in a
minute while alternating between right-hand and left-
hand lay-up positions.

85 – 90   ***Shooting contest:*** Highest point total from shooting from
10 feet away from the basket.

Attachment C

Offensive Play Against Man-to-Man Defense
"The Special"

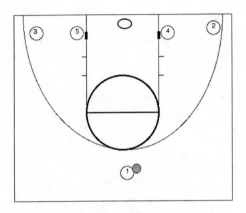

DIAGRAM SPECIAL - A

• Start in "1-4 Low" set. #1
dribbles the ball up the court.

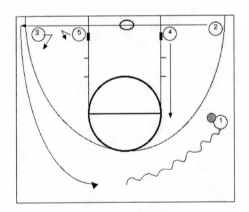

DIAGRAM SPECIAL - B

• #1 dribbles to free throw line
extended near out-of-bounds.
• #2 clears & goes all the way
around to top of the key.
• #4 waits until #1 picks up dribble
& breaks hard to 2 feet above the
elbow.
• #3 & #5 move to keep
defenders occupied.

41

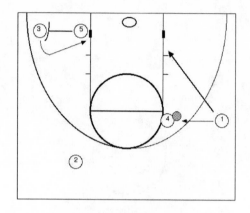

DIAGRAM SPECIAL - C

• #1 passes to #4 and cuts directly to basket at 45% angle.

• #5 sets a pick for #3 to improve rebounding position, and then #5 rolls to the basket for rebounding.

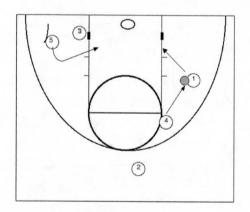

DIAGRAM SPECIAL - D

• #4 bounce-passes to #1 for a lay-up. If #1 is covered, #4 is in triple threat position.
• Why it works:
  - Only 2 passes - not many chances for turnovers.
  - #1's defender's eyes typically follow the flight of the ball and loses sight of player breaking to basket.

Attachment D

Tips for Coaching Shooting Form

- **Assessment of current shooting form** — To coach proper shooting form, it's helpful get an assessment of current shooting technique without your players knowing you're going to be focusing on shooting form. Divide players into two teams and conduct a shooting contest, perhaps dribbling from half-court, players have to dribble to a point (use the free throw line for 7th and 8th graders; further in for younger grades), stop and shoot. First team to make 10 baskets wins. As the players are shooting, make notes about key points to work on with each player.

- **Videotaping** — Consider using a camcorder to capture players' existing shooting form. This can be a valuable exercise. As a coach, you can see things on video by re-watching multiple times that might not show up in live action. As a player, watching yourself on a video provides a unique perspective. When I first saw my golf swing on video, I never realized how much I dipped down before I struck the ball. By seeing myself in action, I immediately knew I needed to make a correction in my golf swing.

- **Approach** — It's helpful to teach shooting form at a practice in which every player has a basketball and the gym has many hoops. There are many facets to teaching good shooting form. Avoid the temptation to try to lecture to your team about all aspects in one sitting. The players will likely be anxious and you'll lose their attention. It's best to break up instructions into bite-size chunks. To accomplish that, alternate between talking to the players at half-court and having them practice the techniques at the hoops or against a wall. After practicing 5 minutes on one specific aspect of shooting, e.g. alignment, players are called in to center court to go over another element, e.g. follow-through. Then, back to the hoops for more practice before being called in again. By rotating instruction with practice, kids will stay interested.

Attachment D, continued

- **Starting off** — When learning proper shooting form, players will sometimes focus too soon on the immediate results — whether the shot went in or not— versus, is the shooting form correct? To at least partially address that, you'll want to let players know that usually when we try some technique for the first time, it's going to feel different and maybe even awkward. Another way to address the same issue is to remove the basketball hoops from the shooting process for the first couple of teaching points. When you teach "how to hold the ball" perhaps you have players just shoot the ball in the air, near center court. When you teach "shooting alignment," perhaps you have players shoot against a wall in the gym first, before moving to the hoops.

- **Diagnostics** — To continue to assess shooting form and corrections that are being implemented, encourage your players to hold their form until the ball either hits the rim or the floor after their shot. By holding their form, you and eventually they, will frequently be able to tell what was done correctly and what wasn't.

- **Key teaching points** (assumes shooter is right-handed):

  How to hold the ball: High school players and older are encouraged to hold the ball with their fingertips. For younger players, this might be very difficult to accomplish. Instead, the focus should be on the placement of the shooting hand being directly behind the ball. To accomplish this, here's a good exercise. Have each player balance the ball in their shooting hand, with the arm extended and their palm of their shooting hand facing the floor. The shooting hand's fingers should be pointed away from the player. Younger players might need to have their off-hand help for balance. From that position, have players flip their right hand into a shooting position with their shooting hand palm facing the floor, but with the player's shooting hand fingers pointing to their right shoulder. It's a quick flip, and the off-hand is needed immediately to grab hold of the ball. If they're able to maintain control of the basketball, the shooting hand should be close to the correct starting position. The left hand's fingers should be placed on the side of the ball with the fingers pointed up.

Shooting Alignment: The player's shooting hand, elbow, knee and toes should be in alignment with the target. To accomplish this, players cannot center the ball at chest level. The alignment is off with that approach. Instead the starting position for the ball is to the shooting hand's side, usually just below the temple. If players are missing shots left or right of the basket, it's usually due to poor alignment.

Starting position for your feet and balance: The foot under your shooting hand should be about a half a foot ahead of your other foot. This will provide you better balance. The foot under your shooting hand should also be the point that you center when you're attempting a free throw. Instead of having the center point be the spot between both feet, it makes sense to align with the ball, shooting hand, elbow, knee and toes (of the foot under the shooting hand). Players need to stay balanced when they shoot. When they jump, they should plan on going straight up and landing in a similar position to where they started. If you see one-foot way ahead of the other after a shot, you can tell the shooting form has been compromised.

Your target: Shooting experts and coaches have differing opinions on what specifically a shooter's eyes should be focused on. Some suggest aiming two inches above the rim. Some suggest focusing on the front of the rim and your body will make the necessary adjustment for the ball to clear the rim. I prefer the latter. Remember the front of the rim changes based on where you're standing on the court. The shooter shouldn't focus on the flight of the ball but rather on the target. Encourage players to use the backboard for shots near 45 degree angles from afar and on lay-ups.

Attachment D, continued

Power: The power for your shots comes from your legs. The farther the shot, the more leg power is needed.

Off-hand release: The off-hand releases the ball after helping control its flight. The ending position of the off-hand should be similar to the starting position, only raised. The palm of the hand faces the same direction upon completion of the shot as it did at the start.

Shooting hand release: The shooting hand follows through to the target as the wrist flicks. The wrist movement gives the ball a backspin rotation. This flip of the wrist is sometimes referred to as "gooseneck" or "hand-in-the-cookie-jar." When diagnosing players' shots, look to see if the shooting hand is aimed exactly at the target after shot has been released. A right-handed shooter's shot hand may sometime stray to the right, almost sideways on release. Work with the shooter to follow through straight to the target. A shooting drill that permits players only to use their shooting hand — start two feet from the basket — is one way for players to focus on the shooting hand release.

Shooting arc: Shots that are missed either long or short are usually due to poor shooting arc. Because of lack of strength, younger players tend to shoot the ball flatter than ideal. Encourage high arcing shots. Amongst the best shooter, the primary determinant of shot success is consistency of arc path.

Pivoting: Most shots start with a pivot of some kind. Work on pivots and jump stops to get better at shooting.

The Driveway Workout

Overview

• Start close and work your way out from the basket shooting.

• Do more than just practice shooting. Work on ball handling, pivoting, rebounding and more.

• Consistency is more important than length. Better to practice 30 minutes three times a week than two hours one time a week.

• Practice doesn't make perfect. Perfect practice makes perfect. After warming up, practice at full game speed.

30 Minutes

1. *Warm-up:* Do some lay-ups to warm up — 3 from the right, 3 from the left and 3 in the middle. Stretch a little. (2 minutes)

2. *Dribble wave drills:* Set up 4 cones about 6 feet apart in a row. Practice dribbling both left-handed and right-handed through the cones. Practice as if someone was guarding you. Work on the following transitions before each cone:
   a. Cross-over
   b. Reverse dribble
   c. The "Butch Lee": back-up a step and then execute a cross-over
   d. Between-the-legs
   e. Behind-the-back (10 minutes)

3. *"Look Ma, one hand drill!":* One-handed shooting drill focusing on form. Keep your elbow in, use proper foot placement, bend your legs and a goose-neck follow-through (all in alignment). Start 3 feet from the front of the rim. Go for swishes with the correct arc. Once you've made 5 shots from the 3 foot mark, back up one foot. When you've made 5 shots from the 4 foot mark, back up to the 5 foot mark; and so on. (3 minutes)

Attachment E, continued

4. **"George Mikan Drill":** Alternate shooting from the right-hand lay-up position to the left-hand lay-up position (45 degree angle, two feet from basket). Keep shooting for one minute and count how many baskets you make. After first drill, rest a minute and then complete again. (3 minutes)

5. **"Square-up Drill":** With your back facing the basket, toss the ball 3-5 feet in the air. Catch the ball after it bounces, square-up and into a triple-threat position by pivoting, and shoot. Rebound and repeat. Work around the basket — about 8 – 10 feet at first — so that you're shooting from the left, from the right and from the middle. Extend the distance as you continue to practice. To work on your rebounding and shooting, practice by tossing an overhead or two-handed pass at the backboard. Jump to rebound, square-up and shoot. Repeat. (4 minutes)

6. **"Stop-and-Pop Shooting":** From 20 feet away from the basket, bounce ball hard off the court, catch it, square-up, take one or two hard dribbles to the basket, stop and shoot. Rebound and repeat. (3 minutes)

7. **Power lay-ups:** From near the free throw lane, between the elbows, start in triple threat position, work on one ball fake and one dribble to a lay-up basket. (2 minutes)

8. **Free throws to cool down:** Shoot 10 free throws. (3 minutes)

Inbounds Play Against a 2-3 Zone
"23"

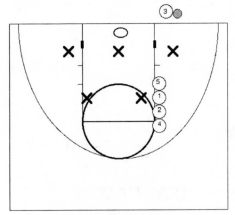

DIAGRAM 23-A

• #3 takes the ball out.

• #5, #1, #2, and #4 stand in line on the same side the ball is being thrown in on.

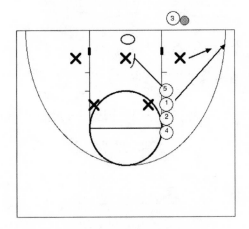

DIAGRAM 23-B

• #5 moves first and effectively sets a pick on the center defender by backing into her looking for the ball.
• #1 moves immediately to the far right hand corner and loudly calls for the ball to attract the nearest defender.

49

Attachment F, continued

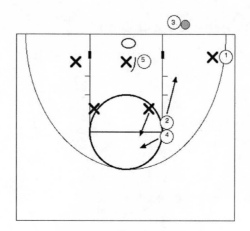

DIAGRAM 23-C

• #4 waits until #1 is almost in the corner and then drops back to the left 3 steps.
• #2 moves into the opening vacated by the wing and the screened out center defender.

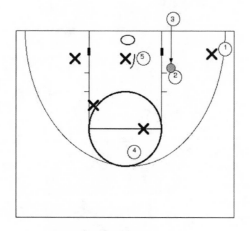

DIAGRAM 23-D

• #3 passes to #2 for a short shot.
• If #2 is covered, #3 looks for #1 or #4.

KEYS TO THE PLAY
• #1 must get wide enough to move the wing defender away.
• The timing of player movement.

50

Attachment G

Inbounds Play Against Man-to-Man
"Pizza"

A simple pick-and-roll play that's easy to teach and surprisingly effective.

Keys to the Play:

• If #1 is open, encourage #3 to use a bounce pass.

• The pass must be delivered on time.

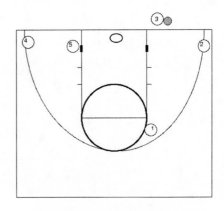

DIAGRAM PIZZA-A

#3 throws in the ball.

#5 and #1 execute a pick-and-roll while #2 AND #4 switch positions.

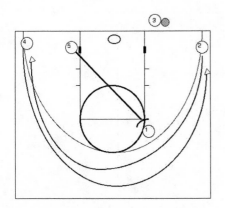

DIAGRAM PIZZA-B

• #5 sets a pick for #1.

• #2 & #4 keep their defenders occupied by taking the long way to change positions.

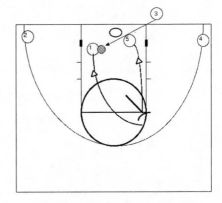

DIAGRAM PIZZA-C

• #1 uses the pick and moves down the left side of the lane looking for a pass.

• #5, after setting the pick, rolls to the basket on the right side.

• #3 passes to #1 or #5.

LaVergne, TN USA
19 March 2010
176594LV00004B/191/A